Cal
Ripken, Jr.

Additional titles in the Sports Reports *series:*

Michael Jordan
Star Guard
(0-89490-482-5)

Jim Kelly
Star Quarterback
(0-89490-446-9)

Chris Mullin
Star Forward
(0-89490-486-8)

Cal Ripken, Jr.
Star Shortstop
(0-89490-485-X)

David Robinson
Star Center
(0-89490-483-3)

Barry Sanders
Star Running Back
(0-89490-484-1)

Thurman Thomas
Star Running Back
(0-89490-445-0)

SPORTS REPORTS

Cal Ripken, Jr.

Star Shortstop

Jeff Savage

ENSLOW PUBLISHERS, INC.

44 Fadem Road   P.O. Box 38
Box 699   Aldershot
Springfield, N.J. 07081   Hants GU12 6BP
U.S.A.   U.K.

Library of Congress Cataloging-in-Publication Data

Savage, Jeff, 1961–
    Cal Ripken, Jr. : star shortstop / Jeff Savage.
      p. cm. – (Sports reports)
    Includes bibliographical references (p.) and index.
    ISBN 0-89490-485-X
    1. Ripken, Cal, 1960– —Juvenile literature. 2. Baseball players—
United States—Biography—Juvenile literature. 3. Baltimore Orioles
(Baseball team)—Juvenile literature. [1. Ripken, Cal, 1960– . 2. Baseball
players.] I. Title. II. Series.
GV865.R47S28 1994
796.357'092—dc20
   [B]   94-5544
                                                   CIP
                                                        AC

Printed in the United States of America

10 9 8 7 6 5

Photo Credits: Baltimore Orioles, pp. 9, 12, 21, 27, 55, 57, 59, 61, 67, 83, 87,
91, 93. Mickey Pfledger, p. 24; Tom Sullivan, pp. 48, 82; Jerry Wachter, pp.
31, 32, 35, 40, 44, 65, 71, 77, 94; Jo Winstead, p. 17.

Cover Photo: Jerry Wachter

Contents

PERMA - BOUND

22.60

3/99

99-739

Chapter 1

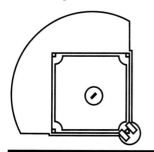

Hitting out of a Slump

Cal Ripken, Jr., arrived at Royals Stadium for the July 1991 doubleheader in a batting slump. The tall Baltimore Orioles shortstop had not gotten a hit in five games. And people were beginning to wonder if Cal had again lost his batting stroke.

"Cal has always had a tendency to slip into some bad habits, get overanxious, and try to do some things he shouldn't be doing," Kansas City pitcher Mike Boddicker said before the doubleheader.[1] Boddicker knew Cal well. He was a former teammate of Ripken's with the Orioles. Boddicker also remembered how Cal struggled at the plate the previous season. In fact, Cal was dropped from third to sixth in the batting order midway through the year. Cal finished the season with 21 home runs and 84 runs batted in, which is fine for just about any baseball player. But Cal Ripken isn't just *any* player! He is an All-Star shortstop, a World Series performer, and a future Hall-of-Famer. His .250 batting average in 1990 was his lowest since joining the major leagues a decade earlier. Cal expected more of himself than his 1990 stats.

Cal stood in the batting cage in Kansas City, taking practice pitches, just as he did before every game. Thousands of fans began to trickle into the massive stadium to take their seats beneath a bright sun. The day would be nice for baseball, but not nice for Cal if he couldn't break out of his slump.

Between each batting practice pitch, Cal thought about the new stance he had learned in the off-season. Manager Frank Robinson had changed Cal's batting technique.[2] Before this, Cal had only taken batting advice from his father—Cal Ripken, Sr.—who was the Orioles' manager until Robinson took over. But Cal junior was so disappointed with his hitting in 1990 that he decided to listen to a fresh voice.

When Cal was a young boy he used to go to Orioles games and watch Frank Robinson rip home runs out of the park. Now that Cal was a star for his favorite team, and Robinson was his manager, Cal trusted his idol to change his swing. The two worked for several weeks during the winter in a room beneath Baltimore's Memorial Stadium.

Cal Ripken has played for the Baltimore Orioles since 1981.

Robinson discovered Cal's feet were too close together. This stance caused Cal to lunge at the ball
with a long stride. Robinson told Ripken to widen
his stance and practice a quick crisp stroke. "What
I did was spread out a little, flexing my batting
stance," Cal said. "Hitting is patience and quick
hands."[3]

After teaching Cal a new batting style, Robinson
explained the mental side of hitting. He told Cal
about one slump during his own career when he
thought he would never get another hit. "You start
to feel alone, as if you're the only one who has ever
gone through it," the manager told Cal.[4]

The batting advice helped Cal. The 1991 season
started off with a bang as Ripken homered in his
first swing during an intra-squad game. He
pounded the ball through spring training and continued to display his new swing and confidence in
the regular season. Against the Texas Rangers in the
fourth game of the season, Cal cracked a single,
triple, and home run in his first four at bats. He
came up again in the ninth inning, needing a double
to hit for the cycle—which means getting each type
of hit in the game. Instead of hitting a double, Cal
walloped a fastball from pitcher Brad Arnsberg
over the center-field wall for his second home run
of the game! Two months later Ripken still led the

American League in home runs and slugging percentage.

As Cal prepared to play the Royals in the doubleheader, he thought his swing seemed to be slipping away. Ripken hadn't gotten a hit in sixteen straight at bats. How could his good swing disappear so quickly? Just a week earlier, Ripken remembered, he was hitting the ball so hard that the Minnesota Twins violated common baseball strategy. The Twins intentionally walked him in the last inning, even though he represented the winning run. The plan backfired on Minnesota. The Orioles' next batter, Randy Milligan, doubled to drive in Ripken and win the game.[5]

In the first game of the doubleheader against the Royals, Cal and the Orioles faced hard-throwing pitcher Kevin Appier. Cal grounded out in the first inning and popped out in the third. His hitless streak had now reached eighteen at bats. In the sixth inning, Cal finally broke through with a single to left field. It was a relief for Cal to finally get a hit.

When he came to the plate again in the eighth inning, the Orioles were trailing, 5–1, with Brady Anderson on first base. Cal ripped a triple off the left-field wall to score Anderson and cut the Kansas City lead to 5–2. Sam Horn followed with a double to send Ripken home and make the game 5–3. Another

To pull him out of a slump, Orioles manager Frank Robinson changed Ripken's batting stance for the 1991 season.

single enabled Horn to score, and the Orioles had closed to within one run. Ripken was beginning to feel his good swing returning. The Royals scored three runs in the bottom of the eighth inning to take an 8–4 lead. The game appeared lost for Baltimore. But the Orioles didn't give up.

In the ninth, David Segui led off with a walk. Then Royals reliever Jeff Montgomery struck out Mike Devereaux. The Royals just needed a double play to win the game. Next at bat, Brady Anderson hit a ground ball that rolled through the middle of the infield for a base hit. Now Cal Ripken was at the plate. Cal already had gotten two straight hits. So he was finally able to relax again at the plate. Cal swung at Montgomery's first pitch and hammered it into left field for a single. The ball was hit so hard that Segui, who was running from second base, had to hold at third. The Orioles now had the bases loaded, needing four runs to tie. Catcher Chris Hoiles came to the plate, representing the tying run. Montgomery delivered a fastball. And Hoiles drilled it deep to left field and high over the wall for a grand slam! The Orioles came running out of the dugout to greet Segui, Anderson, Ripken, and Hoiles. Now the game was tied.

The Royals didn't score in the bottom of the ninth, so the game went into extra innings. Tim

Hulett singled to lead off the tenth for the Orioles. The next two batters made outs, but then Devereaux singled. The Orioles now had runners at the corners (first and third base) with Anderson coming up. Ripken was standing in the on-deck circle, and the Royals knew he was hot. The Kansas City team didn't want to pitch to him again. Montgomery, focusing on Anderson, threw a fastball right down the middle. Anderson jumped on the pitch, driving it deep to center and out of the park for a three-run homer. The Orioles suddenly led the game by three runs! Ripken showed he was back by drilling the next pitch for a double. The Orioles went on to win the game, 11–8.

Cal couldn't wait for the second game of the doubleheader to begin. He had four straight hits—two singles, a double, and a triple. He was hitting the ball hard again, and he wanted to stay in the groove. In the first inning, Cal hit a bullet down the line, but it was snared by the Kansas City third baseman for an out. In his next at bat—in the third inning—Cal drilled a single up the middle, driving in a run. He got another hit in the seventh, and came around to score to give the Orioles a 5–3 lead. Baltimore then stretched the lead to 8–3. But in the eighth inning, Kansas City rallied to tie the game—just as Baltimore did in the first game.

Again, a game had gone into extra innings. By the twelfth inning, the Royals seemed afraid to pitch to Ripken. With one out, they walked him on four pitches. Cal ended up scoring the winning run on consecutive singles by Milligan and Joe Orsulak. The Orioles had won both games of the double-header. Even better for Cal, he had rediscovered his batting stroke.[6]

The Orioles had to play the Indians next, and they didn't get to Cleveland until 3 A.M. the next morning. When the game started, there were plenty of bleary-eyed players in the Orioles dugout. The lack of sleep didn't seem to bother Ripken.

Cal already had one hit when he returned to the plate in the eighth inning. The Orioles trailed by one run, 3–2. Cal hit Rod Nichols' first pitch high over the left-field wall for a game-tying home run. This game also went into extra innings. The Orioles scored twice in the twelfth to win, 5–3. In Boston three days later, Cal homered, and the Orioles won, 7–3. The following night in Boston, Cal homered again, and the Orioles won, 6–4. The next day in Detroit, Cal hit a three-run homer, and the Orioles won again, 10–2.

Cal was still bashing the ball when he showed up a week later in Toronto for the All-Star Game. Cal had hit twenty or more home runs in all ten of his major league seasons, and he had played in the All-Star game nine straight years. But he had yet to hit a home run in an All-Star game. The day before the game, Cal won a homer-hitting contest against some of baseball's top sluggers. The next night, millions of people watched on TV as Cal drilled a three-run homer to give the American League a 4–2 victory.

Cal finished the year with 34 home runs, batting .323. He drove in 114 runs. And he was awarded a Gold Glove for being the best fielding shortstop in the league. Even though the Orioles missed the playoffs, Cal was named the 1991 Most Valuable Player in the American League. Ripken showed that he was able to overcome a frustrating slump in the middle of the year by working hard and not giving up. Perhaps even more impressive than all of that, though, is that Cal played in every game for the entire season—just as he had the previous eight seasons.

More than anything else, Cal Ripken is most famous for "the Streak." Since May 30, 1982, Cal has played in every game for the Orioles. On September 6, 1995, he played in his 2,131st straight game. The record for consecutive games played was set by Lou Gehrig of the New York Yankees. Gehrig played in 2,130 straight games, and was nicknamed the "Iron

FACT

Cal Ripken was officially declared a "Living Legend" by *Sports Illustrated* magazine in 1991. Of the ten athletes chosen, Cal and pitcher Nolan Ryan were the only baseball players. Maybe you'll recognize the other athletes that were selected for this honor: Michael Jordan, Wayne Gretzky, Joe Montana, Jack Nicklaus, Edwin Moses, Carl Lewis, Jimmy Connors, and Martina Navratilova.

Ripken has not sat on the bench since 1982.

Horse" for his durability. No one thought Gehrig's streak could ever be broken. Through dedication and hard work, Cal did. Best of all, he was able to play all those games with his favorite team—the Baltimore Orioles.

Chapter 2

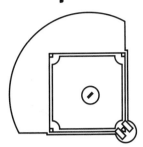

Learning About Baseball

Cal Ripken junior sat on the edge of his chair, staring at the checkerboard. As a six-year-old boy, Cal had just learned how to play checkers. He had challenged the girl next door to a contest, and now they were playing the game in his house. Even at an early age, Cal was very competitive. Before he went next door to challenge the girl, Cal figured out how to trick an opponent at checkers. Now, with the girl sitting across from him, Cal tried his strategy. He set her up for a five-jump move. The girl fell for it, and Cal won the game.

Cal was so excited that he jumped up in the air and banged his head on a concrete windowsill. The gash required stitches. Cal said his head hurt, but he didn't mind so much because he won the game on a great move.[1]

"As a kid, winning was everything," recalled

Cal. "I had to win at all costs. If I lost, I'd throw a tantrum. Playing canasta (a card game), I might get to draw two cards, but sometimes I would cheat and sneak an extra two. So I would win at all costs, but it was never satisfying. I didn't beat them because I was better. I beat them because I cheated. Then, I'd run around saying, 'I'm the champion.'"[2]

Cal's favorite opponent in canasta, or in any other game, was his little brother, Billy. Cal enjoyed competing against Billy because he could usually outsmart him. The two boys often played a game called "sack the quarterback." Cal would win at that game too. "I was the quarterback, and he was the defensive line," Billy recalled. "There was no offensive line. I would snap the ball, and he'd come in and destroy me. Sack the quarterback. . . . He thought it was the greatest game in the world."[3]

Cal was four years older and much bigger than Billy. In any game involving strength, Cal would push his little brother around. Sometimes, though, Cal and Billy would team up. In neighborhood touch football games, Cal would pick Billy to be on his team. Then, with Cal as the quarterback and Billy as the wide receiver, the brothers would connect for touchdown after touchdown. "People would forget about me because I was so small," Billy said.[4]

Cal remembers his biggest dream as a boy was to play pro baseball. Then he wanted to compete in the "Superstars Competition" so he could win at several sports. When Cal was asked a few years ago to compete as a member of the Orioles, he refused to go. "I had no time to prepare," Cal said, "so I didn't go."[5]

As competitive as Cal is, he has the toughness to back it up. As a pro with the Orioles, he hasn't missed a single game in over eleven years. Cal learned early how to be tough. In fact, he grew up in Aberdeen, Maryland, site of the U.S. Army Proving

As a boy, Cal loved competing against his little brother, Billy.

Ground—where tanks and other machinery are tested for toughness.

His father, Cal senior, was a minor league baseball player and then a coach. "My bedtime stories," Cal said, "were about foul tips splintering up fingers, and taping them together, spitting a little tobacco juice on them, and saying to the umpire, 'Let's play.' Hearing those stories, it was like my dad had to break his back to stay out of the lineup."[6]

One winter night in Aberdeen, when Cal was sixteen, a heavy snowfall blocked the road around the Ripken's house. Mr. Ripken bundled up and went outside to rig a plow to an old tractor. Cal junior and little brother, Billy, went out with their dad. The tractor battery went dead, so Mr. Ripken tried to crank the tractor by hand. The crank backfired, and flew up, striking Mr. Ripken in the forehead and opening up a bloody gash. "We've got to go to the hospital, Dad," Cal said. He pleaded with his father, but Mr. Ripken replied, "Just go on home." Mr. Ripken held an oily rag on his forehead, got the tractor started, and plowed the snow off the road.[7]

Cal has another brother named Fred who might be the best athlete in the family. "He would have been perfect returning kickoffs in the NFL," Billy said. "Total disregard for his body. Total." Fred works as a motorcycle mechanic.[8] Cal also has a sister named Ellen, who is the oldest of the children. Ellen is a terrific fast-pitch softball player.

Cal Ripken senior was a minor league catcher for nine years. Then he became a minor league manager in 1961. Cal junior had been born a year earlier, and he doesn't remember a summer when he didn't travel to where his father was managing. Every June after the school year ended, the Ripkens would hitch the trailer to the family car and drive to Rochester, New York, or Dallas, Texas, or Appleton, Wisconsin—or wherever dad was coaching that summer. "We had to leave our friends at home and make new friends along the way," Cal recalled.[9]

Cal's best friends during the summer were his two brothers and his sister. Vi Ripken, Cal's mother, used to teach her children card games, or even invent games, to keep them active. Cal says his mother was the big reason his family was so close. One time when Billy played for Aberdeen High, he pitched a game in freezing weather and wind so strong he was blown off the mound. The only spectator was a woman with a baseball cap pulled over her ears—Mrs. Ripken. "Growing up, I respected my mom and dad very much," Cal said. "The biggest thing they taught me is the difference between right and wrong. That sounds like a very general

Cal and Billy learned the game of baseball by watching their dad coach minor league teams.

sort of thing, but it's amazing how many people don't know the difference."[10]

Something else Cal learned while growing up was baseball. On the days he was home, Mr. Ripken left the house every day at 1 P.M. And when he was coaching on the road, Cal senior was gone for days at a time. Cal junior learned very early that if he wanted to see his father, he would have to go to the ballpark with him. On the drive to the park, Cal junior would ask his dad all sorts of questions about the game of baseball.

At the park Mr. Ripken would put Cal in a miniature uniform and send him to the outfield, saying, "Don't come into the infield, son. It's too dangerous in there. You can get hurt bad. Shag flies or whatever. And always keep your eyes open." Even at the ballpark, Cal wouldn't get to spend much time with his father. But at least he did get to talk with him during the drive to the park. "I liked those drives," Cal said.[11]

When Cal junior was eleven, he remembers saying to himself, "This is what I want to do." From that point on, he worked at improving his skills and studying the game.[12] He played baseball every chance he got. When there wasn't a field nearby, he would create one. Cal and Billy would tape up a ball. Then Cal would use a broomstick for a bat, and

Billy would pitch. One summer the boys played in a yard with a stone wall fence. "Cal would hit it over the fence all the time," Billy remembered. Cal even batted left-handed sometimes, and he would whack it over the fence anyway.[13]

Cal junior began dreaming of playing pro baseball. It didn't necessarily have to be in the big leagues, either. Just as long as it was the pros. "I always figured just in the minors, like my dad," Cal said. "That would have been good enough for me."[14]

Sometimes Cal and his brothers would take batting practice pitches from their father. Mr. Ripken would throw the boys all the pitches he knew—fastballs, curveballs, sliders, and knuckleballs. Cal learned to hit every kind of pitch. At twelve, Cal hit his first ball out of the park. At thirteen, he began wearing his dad's big catcher's mitt and started catching 80-mile-per-hour fastballs from minor league pitchers.

When Cal junior was fifteen, his dad became a coach with the Orioles in Baltimore. Cal was playing baseball for Aberdeen High School at the time. After practice and games, he would hustle over to Memorial Stadium still wearing his uniform. The stadium ticket-takers knew who he was and let him in for free. On weekends, Cal and Billy would go to

Ever since his dad became a coach with the Baltimore Orioles, Cal dreamed of playing professional baseball.

the stadium early. Then they would shag flies with the team and take batting practice from the Orioles' pitching coach.

Cal spent a lot of his time with the Orioles' shortstop Mark Belanger and pitcher Jim Palmer because those were the two positions Cal played at his high school. Belanger would give Cal tips on how to play shortstop—little bits of advice that other kids his age could never get. Palmer, who became a Hall-of-Famer, taught Cal how to throw all sorts of pitches. Cal junior also often talked with other Orioles such as Al Bumbry, Ken Singleton, Bobby Grich, Don Baylor, and Doug DeCinces. Cal's favorite time was after the game in the locker room. "I was like a reporter," he said. "I would review game charts and have all my questions ready. Why did this guy steal? Why didn't the catcher throw on this play? I would fire the questions at my dad. He'd tell me why everything happened. I'd question the player the next day. Why did you do that? What were you thinking?"[15]

Cal junior was learning a great deal about the game of baseball.

Chapter 3

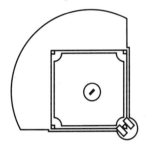

Playing High School Ball

By the time Cal Ripken was a junior, he was the most popular athlete at Aberdeen High. Not only did Cal seem to be a natural athlete, he had also developed a good attitude on the sports field. "I watched Calvin progress from the ninth grade up," said George Connelly. Connelly was a physical education instructor who would become Cal's baseball coach during Ripken's senior year. The coach said, "Cal had good hand-eye coordination and was a great athlete. But more important, he was a good leader and very mature for his years. Calvin could accept things and not lose control of himself if things went badly for him in a ball game. He had the ability to control himself."[1]

One of Cal's favorite sports was soccer, and he played three years for the Aberdeen High Eagles. As a center-halfback, Cal led Hartford County in scoring his senior year, and the Eagles won the county title. "Cal was the team's best player," Connelly remembered. "He wanted to play forward for the basketball team, too, but he couldn't because it was the same season as soccer. He could've played any sport he wanted. I was the football coach and I would've loved Cal to be our quarterback. He would've been an All-League quarterback."

As much as Cal wanted to be the quarterback for the Eagles, he knew he had to focus on baseball if he wanted to make it in the pros. Cal played Little League baseball in North Carolina while his dad was managing at Asheville in the Southern League. Ripken's Little League team won the state title.

Playing on the Aberdeen High baseball team, however, was a different story. Cal had so much potential that coach Don Morrison decided to put him on the varsity team as a freshman. It was a difficult adjustment for Cal. Playing mostly shortstop, Cal batted under .200 for the season. His sophomore season wasn't much better, as he hit just over .200. But Cal's fielding was fine, thanks to the advice he was getting from Orioles' shortstop Mark Belanger. Cal knew, though, that he had to hit the ball much better to be drafted by a pro team. He often sought comfort from his father. "Every once in a while, I'd go to him for a confidence builder, to make me feel better," Cal said. "He wouldn't do it. He'd say, 'You're not hitting the ball the way you can.'" Mr. Ripken would always tell Cal the same two words: "Keep battling."[2]

Cal grew in size, and came back for his junior season as a bigger stronger player. He was faster too, able to run from home plate to first base in 4.1 seconds. The coach picked Cal as the team's number-one starting pitcher, and the players voted him a co-captain of the team. Cal's fastball wasn't great, but he had excellent control and almost never

Although he liked to play many sports, Cal knew he had to focus on baseball to make it in the pros.

walked batters. When he didn't pitch, he played shortstop almost flawlessly. He also greatly improved his hitting, finishing the season with a batting average above .300. In recognition of his performance, Cal was named to the All-Hartford County team. The only outcome Cal was disappointed with was his team's loss in the playoffs. Cal wanted to win the county title. He returned for his senior season determined to do just that.

George Connelly replaced Don Morrison as coach for Cal's final season at Aberdeen. Cal

Cal played as both a pitcher and a shortstop for his high school team.

opened the season with a bang against John Carroll High, going 5-for-5 at the plate and driving in five runs. When the Eagles lost three of their next six games, however, Cal became concerned. As team captain, Cal called a meeting and declared that every single player, including Cal himself, must play as hard as possible on every play. The team didn't lose again the rest of the season.

Cal alternated between pitcher and shortstop, and led the county in hitting all year. He batted .492 for the season, with 29 RBIs in just 20 games. He slugged 4 home runs, but could have hit more if the ballfields in Hartford County had fences. Outfielders would stand so deep that sometimes they would catch balls that Cal hit nearly 400 feet. "He would have had at least 10 homers if the fields weren't open," coach Connelly said. As a pitcher, Cal finished the year with a 7–2 record and an amazing 0.70 earned-run average. He struck out 100 batters in just 60 innings. The Eagles reached the Maryland Class A state title game with a 17–3 record.[3]

Baltimore Orioles scouting director Tom Giordano watched Ripken pitch several times and said his delivery looked like Jim Palmer's. No wonder, since Palmer helped teach Cal how to pitch. "I've never seen a high school kid throw a better change-up," the scout said.[4]

The state title game was held on a cloudy Saturday at Prince Georges Community College near Washington, D.C. The Eagles squared off against Thomas Stone High. Ripken pitched for Aberdeen even though he had only two days of rest from his last playoff start. The Eagles fell behind early, 3–1, but it began to rain. By the bottom of the fourth inning, the rain was pouring so hard that the umpires declared a rainout and rescheduled the game. Afterward Cal said, "My fastball wasn't working and I had control problems. But that doesn't mean we would have lost. We were only two runs down and this is a good hitting club. We can come back on any club."[5]

The title game was rescheduled for Wednesday, but now Cal had something else on his mind. The baseball amateur draft would be Tuesday, the day before the game. How could he concentrate? Several clubs said they were interested in drafting Ripken. Cal, of course, hoped he would be picked by the Orioles. He had grown up around the team. His friends were there, and so was his father. There were twenty-six major league teams, though, and the odds weren't good that Cal would be selected by Baltimore.

But the Orioles weren't about to let Cal slip

The Orioles had enough confidence in Cal's batting and pitching abilities to draft him for their minor league team right out of high school.

away. In the second round of the draft the team selected Cal, saying they liked his potential and enthusiasm for the game. They decided right then that even though Cal was a good pitcher, he would be more valuable as an infielder because he could play every day, not just every five days. Cal was very excited. He said right away that he would join the Orioles' minor league system, rather than attend college. "It may be my only chance to play pro ball, so I don't want to miss out," he said. "But I do hope to go to college in the off-season."[6]

Cal couldn't wait to show the Orioles that they didn't make a mistake drafting him so early. The next day, in the title game against Thomas Stone, Cal was amazing. In the first inning, Cal struck out the side. Still, Thomas Stone scored a run on an error to take a 1–0 lead. In the second inning, Cal struck out two more batters. In the third he needed only eleven pitches to set the Lions down in order, and got two more strikeouts in the process.

The Eagles rallied in the top of the fourth to take a commanding lead. With one out, five Aberdeen players in a row got on base. First, Glen Gillis reached on an error. Next, Tony Canami was hit by a pitch. Then when Steve Hinch hit a grounder up the middle, the Thomas Stone defense couldn't make a play because Canami upended the shortstop on a hard slide. Gillis ended up scoring on the play to tie the game, 1–1. The fourth batter, Dave Bonsali, followed with a single to score Canami for a 2–1 lead. Finally Ripken, hitting third in the order, followed with a single to load the bases. After the second out John Waldon walked, forcing in another run to make the score 3–1. Next, Cory Marshall singled to drive in the fourth run. Then Mark Barnes followed with another single to drive in Ripken and give Aberdeen a 5–1 lead. Two more Eagles came around to score on a throwing error, and suddenly the game was 7–1.

Thomas Stone High came back in the bottom of the fourth to score a run on two hits, cutting the lead to 7–2. But these would be the only two hits Ripken would allow in the game. Cal hit two balls over 350 feet, but both were caught near the wall. His pitching was even better, as he finished the game with 17 strikeouts. He struck out at least two batters in every inning, and struck out the side in the first, fourth, and fifth. Afterward, Lions coach Ron Stover said, "We didn't hit the ball well, and you can't score if you don't get on base. Ripken is a heck of a pitcher."[7]

Veteran scout Joe Consoli of the major league scouting bureau was quite impressed with Ripken. "He'll be in the big leagues in a few years," Consoli said.[8] The scout knew what he was talking about.

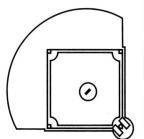

Chapter 4
Making It in the Big Leagues

One week after Cal led his high school team to the state championship, he signed a contract to play for the Orioles. Cal had long admired Baltimore's great third baseman, Brooks Robinson. Robinson retired the previous year after playing his entire career with the Orioles. Cal wanted to become another Brooks Robinson.[1]

A week later Cal was in Bluefield, West Virginia, where the Orioles rookie league team plays. Cal was only seventeen, and living away from home was a difficult adjustment. Cal immediately became Bluefield's starting shortstop and he was very nervous. Through the first fifteen games of the season, Ripken committed so many errors that many people were wondering how he had ever been picked so high in the draft. Teammates began making jokes about Ripken's fielding ability, and he began to doubt himself.

A few minor adjustments were made by coach Wilbert Miner, and soon Cal began to make the plays a second-round draft choice was supposed to. Suddenly the jokes stopped, and so did the errors. By the end of the season, Ripken was ready to be promoted to Single-A Miami. "I remember when I first got down here in June," Cal told a reporter, "I expected everyone here to be a pro, better than me. I remember that I was scared to death."[2] Cal was relieved to survive such a horrible start.

Cal batted just .264 in the rookie league without hitting a home run. He wondered if he would ever hit a homer again. At Miami the following season, he finally got one. And it couldn't have come at a better time. Miami was stuck in a scoreless tie with the West Palm Beach Expos when Cal came up to bat. There were two outs in the twelfth inning, and Expos starter Gary Abone was still pitching. Ripken slammed Abone's first pitch over the wall in left field for the winning run. Cal hit four more homers for Miami that year, batted over .300, and was named to the Topps Class A All-Star team. Midway through the year Miami's regular third baseman suffered an injury. The injury left Miami with two shortstops and no third baseman. Ripken was switched to third. After one of the first shots hit down the third-base line struck him in the throat,

Cal began fielding the ball cleanly at third. Suddenly he was making diving plays, the kind that are thrilling. Later in his career, he admitted, "I felt more at home there."[3] Before the season ended Cal was promoted as a third baseman from Single-A Miami to Double-A Charlotte, in North Carolina.

The first day of batting practice at Charlotte, Cal pounded several balls out of the park. He thought to himself, "Boy, the ball just jumps out of here compared to Miami." But hitting homers wasn't the best plan for Ripken to start thinking about. Trying to hit every pitch out of the park, he changed his swing and began uppercutting the ball. As a result,

Ripken tags the runner out at third. During his first few years in the minor leagues, Ripken played third base.

he started out 0 for 15. The slump continued until the team went on a late-season road trip. "I finally shook out of it," Cal recalled, "but by the time we got back home for a series, the season was over." Cal clubbed three home runs for Charlotte, but he managed only 11 hits in 61 at bats for a .180 batting average.[4]

The following season, he decided to just let the home runs happen, instead of trying to bash the ball. This strategy worked much better, as Cal cracked 25 home runs to break the club record. He was an easy choice for the Southern League's All-Star team. When Cal began his Single-A season in Miami two years earlier, he was 6 feet 4 inches, but weighed just 180 pounds. Now he was up to 205 pounds, and most of it was muscle. The Orioles felt Cal was ready to move up to Triple-A Rochester, one step away from the big leagues. Cal thought so too.

Cal began the 1981 season in Rochester by cracking two homers his first week. Then, in late April, he had the game of his life. He showed up at Silver Stadium early for batting practice, as did several of his teammates. Cal cared so much for his teammates that he volunteered to pitch batting practice to them before he took his cuts in the batting cage. The trouble was, by the time his teammates finished batting practice, there was no time left for Cal. It turns out, he didn't need the practice.

Facing Charleston pitcher Mike Paxton in the third inning, Ripken blasted a fastball over the left-field wall for a home run to tie the game, 1–1. With a runner on base in the sixth, he drilled a curveball out of the park for his second homer of the night. Then in the seventh, Paxton's fastball wasn't fast enough for Ripken. Cal crushed the ball out of the park for his third home run of the game. It was the first three-homer game ever for Cal at any level. "Rip just has great talent, it's as simple as that," Charlotte coach Doc Edwards said after the game. "He just doesn't guess on a pitch. He can figure out a pitcher's pattern."[5]

Cal continued his torrid hitting, and by August he had 23 home runs and 75 RBIs to his credit. He would later be voted the International League Rookie of the Year, and be picked as the top major league prospect. Even though the season had not yet ended, the Orioles could no longer keep Cal down in the farm system. On August 8, 1981, Cal Ripken was called up to the major leagues.

Memorial Stadium in Baltimore had been Cal's playground as a kid. He knew every square foot of the ballpark. When he arrived at the stadium for his first game, he knew exactly where to go. He knew how to get to the clubhouse; he knew which tunnel went to the dugout; he knew how to find the coaches' office, the press box, and the trainer's room. It was as though nothing had changed at Memorial Stadium since Cal was fifteen. What *was* different to Cal this time was that he couldn't just run around and have fun—playing baseball was his new job. And his dad was one of his coaches. Manager Earl Weaver, who always called Cal "kid," would be his boss. So the situation was different than when he was fifteen.

Two days after Cal joined the Orioles, he made his major league debut against the Royals. Weaver sent him into the game as a pinch-runner for Ken Singleton, but Cal didn't score. At Memorial Stadium six days later, Cal got his first major league hit—a single off White Sox pitcher Dennis Lamp. Cal didn't get too many chances to hit after that. His full rookie season would begin the following year, and Cal said he would be ready. The Orioles obviously believed him. Before the 1982 season the team traded third baseman Doug DeCinces. Cal would become the Orioles' new third baseman.

Opening day of the 1982 season arrived and Ripken proved he was ready. He singled as well as got his first major-league double, RBI, and home run—all off Kansas City pitcher Dennis Leonard.

Cal went 3-for-5 on the day, and Baltimore fans were excited about their new star.

Suddenly, though, Cal plunged into a deep slump. He got just four hits in his next 55 at bats. After 18 games Cal's batting average was just .117. Some fans and writers began to say that Cal was on the team only because his father was a coach. Earl Weaver kept telling Cal that his play would improve. But Cal worried that he wouldn't be good enough to make it in the big leagues. He began to get defensive, lashing out at critics who claimed Cal

Cal Ripken, Sr., watches as his son makes a triple. Because of a slump during his rookie season, critics speculated that Ripken was in the starting lineup because his dad was a coach.

Ripken senior was keeping Cal junior in the starting lineup because he was his son. "There is no favoritism in the big leagues," Cal junior said. "Either you cut it or you don't."[6] During a game in May, slugger Reggie Jackson of the Angels pulled Cal aside for a moment and gave the rookie some advice. "Hey kid," Jackson said. "You're pressing too hard. Don't try to be Babe Ruth. Just be yourself. Do what Cal Ripken can do."[7] Cal realized he had been putting too much pressure on himself. He decided right then to try and relax. The next day Cal got two hits. From the Angels dugout Jackson gave him the thumbs-up sign. The day after that Cal got two more hits. He was on his way. By the middle of June, Ripken had played forty-four straight errorless games at third base, and his hitting had become solid. The critics began to quiet, sit back, and watch the rookie phenomenon.

Legendary coach Casey Stengel, understanding the importance of defense, once said: "I don't like them fellas who drive in two runs and let in three." Baltimore manager Earl Weaver agreed. "Let's not give them any more outs than they're entitled to," Earl was fond of saying.[8] Since Earl also knew that defense was important and that shortstop was the most important position, he decided to make a switch. On July 1, 1982, he penciled in Ripken's name at shortstop. He didn't even tell Ripken of the move.

Infielder Lenn Sakata approached Cal in the locker room before the game. "You seen the lineup card," Sakata said to Cal. Ripken said he hadn't. "You're at shortstop," Sakata told him. "I am?" Cal said in disbelief. "Yep," Sakata told him. For the next eight years, Ripken started every game for the Orioles at shortstop. At 6 feet 4 inches, he is the tallest shortstop ever to regularly play the position in the major leagues.

After a couple of early mistakes at his new position, Ripken was worried. Weaver quickly stepped in to give him some advice. He told Cal, "Field it smoothly. Throw it accurately. And if they beat it out, then it's a hit, not an error, and it doesn't bother me."[9] The position switch seemed to help the Orioles. From the day Ripken moved to shortstop until the end of the year, the Os went 56–35—a winning percentage of .615—the best in baseball. Still the team missed making the playoffs by one game.

Ripken led all rookies with 28 homers and 93 RBIs. He raised his batting average to .264—a great improvement from what it had been in early May. The newspaper writers who cover the American League selected Cal as the Rookie of the Year.

Cal learned more about baseball his rookie season than he ever has before or since. First he learned the thrill of playing in big league stadiums, and the frustration of sitting on the bench. He described to a writer the feeling of batting in a pressure situation. "You're at the plate with 50,000 fans on their feet screaming, and it's totally quiet in your mind. When you hit the ball and start running, about halfway to first the sound comes back into your head. There's no better feeling."[10] Cal played in 160 of the Orioles' 162 games. The two that he missed were very frustrating. "I'm competitive," he said. "I always thought I was beyond rest. And sitting on the bench is the worst time of my life.[11]

During his first year with the Orioles, Cal also learned that it was best for him to sometimes stay at the ballpark until 2 or 3 A.M. He was so popular with fans that if he were angry with himself after a game, he didn't want to be near anyone, especially children who looked up to him. He also realized it was best not to say anything bad to a teammate who may have blown the game, especially right away. He said he learned this strategy from his father. The mental part of the game is probably the area where Cal is his strongest.

"You don't want to say something stupid," Cal explained. "My dad's policy is not to say anything

FACT

Cal won the American League Rookie of the Year honors in 1982 by one of the widest margins ever. He out-polled both Kent Hrbek of the Twins and Wade Boggs of the Red Sox. Cal received twenty four of a possible twenty eight first-place votes— far more than Hrbek, who finished second.

to the person until the next day. Usually he felt just as bad about blowing it. Dad figured you didn't accomplish anything by saying something right away. Let the other guy think about it and learn from his mistake. I just used that idea when I decided not to leave here mad. The idea is that cooler heads prevail."[12]

Attitude goes a long way in determining the value of a baseball player, or anybody else, for that matter. The Orioles realized early that Ripken would soon become the team's most valuable player. When Earl Weaver retired after the 1982 season, a lot of the players wanted Cal's dad to

By playing with star veteran players on the Orioles, Ripken learned the value of teamwork his rookie season.

become the new manager. Instead the Orioles gave Joe Altobelli the job. Cal could have complained, but he didn't. "I've never played for Joe," Cal said, "but I like him as a person. I'm almost certain we'll win with him. It will be humorous if we get off to a good start. It would drive Earl crazy."[13] Cal showed the Orioles that not only was he a good hitter and fielder, but he was a classy person as well.

After the season ended, a columnist for the *Baltimore Sun* named Bob Maisel wrote, "One of the things you have to like most about Cal Ripken is the way he takes everything in stride without getting too high on himself or too far down. His easy-going, yet sensible, approach to things involving his career is one of the many reasons you can see nothing but success ahead for him."[14]

Chapter 5

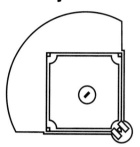

Highs and Lows

The 1983 season opened for Baltimore with Joe Altobelli as the new manager. The Orioles had plenty of talent, but some of the players weren't sure of Altobelli. The manager was sure of one fact though. He knew his tall shortstop was the best in baseball. "Cal Ripken is a rarity, not an oddity," Altobelli said in reference to Cal's height. "He's just a natural athlete. If he'd been playing for the Colts he'd have caught the touchdown pass with 30 seconds left to play. Red Auerbach (Boston Celtics owner) would have lit up more [victory] cigars if he played basketball."[1] Unfortunately for pro football and pro basketball, Cal played baseball. And in 1983 he played it as well as anyone ever has for the Orioles.

With Cal batting third in the lineup and first baseman Eddie Murray batting fourth, the Orioles cruised to the American League East title. Cal came through with his bat at the most important time—during the stretch run. From mid-August until the end of the season, Cal hit .391 with 14 doubles, 9 homers, 30 RBIs, and 40 runs scored.

Cal was the American League Rookie of the Year in 1982, and now his team was going to the playoffs. Could baseball be any more fun? Yes! In the American League playoffs, Cal led the Orioles past the Chicago White Sox. In the first game, Cal singled to drive in a run in the ninth inning against LaMarr Hoyt. But the Orioles lost, 2–1. Cal watched from first base as the Chicago players celebrated their victory. Cal decided it was time for his team to show its toughness.

In the next game, Chicago pitcher Rich Dotson drilled Cal in the ribs with a fastball. Ripken refused to show that he was hurt by rubbing the bruise. Then, when he got to first base, he yelled to Dotson on the mound, "Is that as hard as you can throw?"[2] The next time he faced Dotson, Cal slammed a double. He didn't forget Dotson the following year, either, drilling two homers off him, and hitting .440 against all White Sox pitchers. Facing the White Sox in the 1983 playoffs, Cal collected 6 hits, scored 5 runs, and drove in 2 more to lead Baltimore. The Os beat Chicago three games to one.

99-739

By defeating Chicago in the playoffs the Orioles earned the right to play in the World Series, where they met the Philadelphia Phillies of the National League. As the pre-game introductions of the players were being made on TV, the cameras were pointed at Ripken. ABC commentator Reggie Jackson said, "Ripken had a great year. It very well could be a career year. He might never accomplish this again."[3]

Cal didn't have a particularly good Series at the plate, with just 3 hits in 18 at bats. In the end, though, the Orioles didn't need his bat. Starting pitchers Scott McGregor, Dennis Martinez, Mike Boddicker, and Storm Davis held the Phils to nine runs as Baltimore won the Series in five games. Cal did grab the spotlight, however, in the final game. Baltimore needed just one more out to win the title when Philadelphia's Garry Maddox hit a line drive toward left field. Ripken reached out and caught the liner, and the Orioles were World Champions. They celebrated by riding in a ticker-tape parade through downtown Baltimore.

After the miraculous season Cal was chosen as the Most Valuable Player in the American League. He deserved it by leading the majors in hits—211, which broke the Baltimore team record. He also led the league in runs scored, with 121; and doubles, with 47. He hammered 27 home runs and had 102 RBIs. After winning the award Cal was typically humble, saying, "That was exciting, but it makes you feel a little more important than maybe you are."[4]

At this point in Cal's baseball career, the game seemed easy. He enjoyed so much success that he really didn't know what it was like *not* to win. He was about to find out, though, as the Orioles didn't return to the playoffs for more than a decade. Later in his career, Cal would look back to his early years when he was surrounded in the lineup with hitters such as Eddie Murray, Al Bumbry, Gary Roenicke, John Lowenstein, and Ken Singleton. "I was just a cog on the team, helping the offense run," Cal would say.[5]

The 1984 season for Ripken was much like the previous one. He finished third in the American League in hits, with 195; third in extra base hits, with 71; and ninth in batting, with a .304 average. That average was even better with runners in scoring position. He led all major league shortstops with 27 home runs and 86 RBIs. His hitting was so consistent that he went only as long as three games without a hit just once the entire year.

In the field, Cal broke the all-time record for assists (outs he helped make), with 583. Still, for all

FACT

There have been only two Orioles to have ever hit for the cycle—collecting a single, double, triple, and home run in the same game. Brooks Robinson, Cal's boyhood idol, accomplished the feat in Chicago on July 15, 1960. Cal hadn't even been born yet! On May 6, 1984, at Arlington Stadium in Texas, Cal hit for the cycle—just like his hero.

his personal accomplishments, there wasn't much for Cal to fondly look back on. Baltimore's record of 85–77 wasn't nearly good enough to make the playoffs. The Detroit Tigers raced out to a big lead and wound up beating out the Orioles by 19 games. Cal had to watch the playoffs on TV this time. He watched the Tigers beat the Royals in the playoffs and the Padres in the World Series.

By now Cal was widely recognized as a star. Popular baseball writer Thomas Boswell wrote in the April 1985 issue of *Gentleman's Quarterly* magazine, "Cal Ripken is the best player in baseball. He is the best in the game by a clear margin."[6] Ripken's picture was appearing on the cover of several magazines, including *GQ*. Underneath was the caption: "Cal Ripken is the Best Baseball Player Alive. Period."

Buying and selling baseball cards had become quite popular by this time. In the summer of 1985 a Baltimore card dealer took a trip to the West Coast, hoping to acquire a lot of Ripken cards cheap. He returned to Baltimore disappointed. "Cal Ripken is one of the hottest cards in the country right now," the dealer said.[7]

In May, Ripken played in his 464th consecutive game. This broke the Baltimore record held by former third baseman Brooks Robinson, who was Cal's favorite player. Ripken almost didn't break the record, however. On the second day of the 1985 season—against the Texas Rangers—Cal was in his usual shortstop position, and Gary Ward was on second base for the Rangers. Cal moved forward toward second base for a pickoff play, and his spikes got caught on top of the bag. "I heard a pop, felt the bang," Cal said. "I said, 'That's it, it's broken.'" Orioles trainer Richie Bancells taped Cal's left ankle up tight, and he led off the next inning.

The following day Cal's ankle swelled up like a balloon. Cal probably wouldn't have been able to

Although the Orioles have not made the playoffs since 1983, Ripken is the most famous shortstop in baseball.

play, but the Orioles had the day off. His ankle was not broken, and the swelling went down, so Ripken played in the next game. "The Streak" continued. By the end of the 1985 season, Cal not only had played in 603 games in a row, he hadn't even missed an inning. That's 5,445 straight innings without leaving the field. Cal had another good year at the plate, hitting .282, with 26 homers and 110 RBIs. He hit .321 with runners in scoring position, and was first or second on the Orioles in twelve offensive categories.

By now Cal was making plenty of money. Even though he had become financially successful, he never forgot that he came from a regular family who had to be careful with its money. Cal did what he could to take care of his parents, and then he began to give back to the community. He made a significant contribution to a local daycare center for retarded children. He gave a lot of money to the School for Performing Arts in Baltimore. He bought 25 tickets for every Orioles home game, to be used by underprivileged kids and senior citizens.[8]

Cal also took care of himself. He had a state-of-the-art home gym built in a separate wing of his home in Reisterstown, Maryland. The gym was 30 feet in height and featured a regulation full-sized basketball court, a 60-foot-long lighted batting cage, and a weight room filled with dumbbells, barbells, and machines. "It's like having your own high school gym, without the bleachers," Ripken said.[9]

Cal was proud of his streak of consecutive games. He knew that if he wanted to keep the streak going, he would have to keep fit. Cal talked at length with pitcher Nolan Ryan and catcher Carlton Fisk—both of whom extended their careers several years by properly exercising in the off-season. Using the advice of Ryan and Fisk, Cal developed a conditioning routine that he still uses today.

Ripken donates part of his salary to the community. He gives away twenty-five tickets to every Orioles home game to underprivileged kids.

The routine includes three to four hours of exercise

a day, six days a week. Cal lifts weights four times a week, working his upper body on Monday and Thursday, and his lower body on Tuesday and Friday. One technique he doesn't do is to try to "max out"—to lift as much weight as possible. "I don't get into an ego thing about being the strongest man in the gym," Cal said. "I don't want to tear down a good thing." Three days a week Ripken spends almost an hour working on his baseball skills, such as hitting, fielding, and throwing. To practice fielding, he throws a tennis ball hard and low against a wall and tries to stop it as it shoots back at him.[10]

As good as Cal had become, the Orioles had gotten worse. The glory days of the 1970s and early 1980s were long gone. In 1986, even though Cal had another solid year hitting and fielding, the Orioles suffered through a miserable season. Cal led the club in runs, with 98; hits, with 177; doubles, with 35; and homers, with 25. He led all American League shortstops for the fourth straight year in homers, RBIs, runs, and slugging percentage. He tied New York Yankees first baseman Don Mattingly in game-winning hits, with 15. But the rest of the Orioles didn't help enough. Baltimore suffered its first losing season in nineteen years by finishing the season with a 73–89 record.

Still, Cal was as popular as ever. Midway

through the 1986 season, a magazine put Cal's picture on the cover with the headline: "Cal Ripken, Jr.—One of the Good Guys." In the magazine article Cal explained how he handles pressure. "It's all in how you look at it," Cal said. "I enjoy the pressure situation. It makes you concentrate; it makes your natural abilities come out a little bit more." The night after making this comment, Cal stepped to the plate and belted a three-run homer—the 100th of his career. He drove in four runs to lead the Orioles to a 9–1 victory.[11]

The Orioles weren't winning enough, however. Changes needed to be made. Baltimore started with

To keep "The Streak" of consecutive games going, Ripken keeps fit by exercising and practicing his baseball skills every day.

FACT

Cal Ripken and his brother Billy became the first pair of brothers to hit home runs in the same game in sixteen years. They accomplished the feat at the SkyDome in Toronto on September 16, 1990. Even more impressive is the fact that both Ripkens hit their homers in the same inning—the fifth—off Blue Jays pitcher David Wells. The last pair of brothers to turn the trick was Graig and Jim Nettles in 1974. Graig and Jim, though, were on different teams. The last time two brothers on the same team homered in the same inning was 1962—when all-time home-run king Hank Aaron and brother Tommy did it for the Atlanta Braves.

its entire coaching staff. They decided to make Cal Ripken senior the new manager. They also brought up a new second baseman from the minors, a kid named Billy Ripken—Cal's little brother. For the Ripken family, it was like a dream come true. Cal Ripken senior became the third man in baseball history to manage his son, joining the Macks (Connie and Earl) and the Berras (Yogi and Dale). But no one ever managed *two* sons before this.

It was important that the other players understood right away that Mr. Ripken wouldn't give his sons any special favors. One of the manager's first rules was that, around the ballpark, his sons did not call him "Dad." Cal told reporters in spring training that there wouldn't be any problem with having three family members wearing the same uniform. "From a family perspective it's pretty exciting," Cal said. "But it's no problem on the professional level. Dad taught us to approach it that way, because he always did. There's no favoritism. Some people may think Billy is here because Dad is the manager, but that's not true. We all have a job to do."[12]

Cal and Billy still managed to find some time to play together, just as they did growing up. During spring training in Florida, well before the games were to start, the brothers often played hockey in the locker room with a taped-up ball and a bat. In fact, they would play anything as long as it involved competition. On the practice field, they would run wind sprints together, not to see who would win, but just to be close. "I've dreamed of playing with Billy," Cal said. "I'd like us to be like Alan Trammell and Lou Whitaker in Detroit—so good, so close, so important to the club."[13] During practice Cal would take his grounders at shortstop while Billy would take his at second base. It was obvious early in spring training that Billy tried to copy Cal. Billy admitted as much when he told

Playing on the same team as his younger brother Billy was a dream come true for Cal.

reporters, "You don't see us too far apart on the field. He's giving me, well, the All-Star advice. He's teaching me to do everything."[14]

The Ripkens couldn't wait for the regular season to start. Their dream had actually become a reality.

Chapter 6

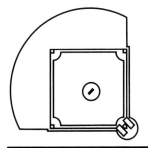

The Lows Get Lower

The Orioles began the 1987 season competitively. Cal opened the season at shortstop, and Billy started at second base. They worked well together in the field, making several double plays. By the middle of May, Cal was hitting .326, with 8 homers and 34 RBIs. During one stretch he went 9 for 25—and all 9 hits were for extra bases (four doubles, a triple, and four homers). Midway through the year, more than 200 players, managers, coaches, and general managers were polled on a number of subjects, including "smartest defensive player." The winner was Cal Ripken.[1]

Cal's batting average took a dive, however. He finished the season hitting just .252. He did knock out 27 home runs and drive in 98 RBIs to lead the club, but the batting average was not typical of Cal. Billy was worse, and at one point, his father had to bench Billy for a while—just as he would any other player. The Os finished with a terrible record of 67–95. Many people were wondering if the Baltimore organization did the right thing in selecting Cal Ripken senior as manager.

One factor that was accepted without question was the durability of the Baltimore shortstop. Cal was not only playing in every game, he was playing in every inning of every game. In fact, from June 5, 1982, until September 14, 1987, Ripken never sat down for a pinch-hitter or a defensive replacement. And he never got hurt. He played in 8,243 innings in a row! That is a major league record that may never be broken.

In the off-season Cal married Kelly Geer. Cal's father served as the best man. The couple would later have a daughter named Rachel and a son named Ryan.

The 1988 season began even worse than the 1987 season ended. The Orioles lost their first six games of the year. Then came the bad news: Cal Ripken senior was being fired. He would return to his old job as the third-base coach. The new manager was Frank Robinson, a Hall-of-Fame outfielder who started for Baltimore in the 1960s. It was a devastating blow to Cal and Billy, but the two middle infielders continued playing as hard as they could.

"I just have to block my personal feelings out of my mind," Cal said. "I just have to keep playing to win. I have to act like a professional."[2]

The managerial change didn't seem to help. The Orioles lost the first game with Robinson as manager. Then during their eighth game, in Kansas City, the Royals set a club record with seven consecutive hits while scoring nine runs in the first inning. The Baltimore losing streak was at eight and counting. The team lost four more in a row at home, and at 0–12, Baltimore was one loss away from tying an

After a dismal season in 1987, the Orioles moved Cal Ripken, Sr., from general manager to third-base coach.

84-year-old record for the worst start ever by a major league team.

The team went on another road trip and continued to lose. By the end of April, the Orioles had lost a record twenty-one straight games to begin the season. Maybe it was not Mr. Ripken's fault after all. Finally, on April 29, the Os finally won. Naturally, Cal led the way with four hits and three runs scored. Eddie Murray hit a homer in the first inning to get the Orioles started. The team went on to thump the Chicago White Sox, 9–0. The agonizing drought finally was over. "Nothing could be worse than this," Cal told reporters afterward. He was right, but not by much.[3]

The losing streak may have been broken, but the Orioles continued to lose more than they won. After forty games the team was 6-34—the worst record any club ever had that late in a season. They finished the year at 54-107—the worst record of any major league team in the decade! The 107 losses were the tenth most in American League history. The Mets won more games at home than Baltimore won in total. The Orioles spent every single day of the season in last place. When the Os left Toronto on the final day of the season, they had finished 23 1/2 games behind the sixth-place team. It was a terrible year. And how did Cal Ripken perform? How

As the Orioles remained in last place for the duration of the 1988 season, Ripken fell into one of the worst batting slumps of his career.

else—he clubbed 23 homers, drove in 81 runs, and scored 87 himself. He also signed a three-year contract in July for $2.45 million a year.

Baltimore's ownership was happy to keep Cal in the organization. After the terrible 1988 season, however, the other highly-paid players had to go. The Los Angeles Dodgers in 1989 had the highest player payroll. The Orioles soon would have the lowest. First the team traded ace pitcher Mike Boddicker. Then they traded cleanup-hitting first baseman Eddie Murray. Cal was crushed. Not only did he and Murray form a potent three-four punch, but Eddie was his best friend on the team (besides his little brother Billy, of course). "We had some good years, some great years," Murray said when he left. "But things went bad, and I got blamed."[4] Cal agreed. But just as he did when his father was fired as manager the year before, Cal had to try to focus on a new year. At least he still had his brother at second base and his dad in the third-base coaching box.

When the 1989 season started, Ripken was the only member of the 1983 World Champion Orioles still with the team. Winning the title seemed so far away now. Cal got off to a slow start at the plate, mostly because there were no big hitters left in the Baltimore lineup. So pitchers would give Cal very few good pitches to hit. Cal was willing to take his share of walks, but he also felt he should earn his large salary by hitting the ball. Instead he wound up swinging at a lot of bad pitches.

The Orioles surprisingly were winning their share of games. The victories began on Opening Day with a win over hard-throwing Roger Clemens and the Boston Red Sox. One-third of the way through the season, the team found itself in first place in the American League East. This number-one position was mostly due to the team's defense. In May the Baltimore infielders made just three errors. The team had allowed a total of just six unearned runs all year. Leading the way were Cal and Billy. In July, with the Orioles still in the race, the team took a 5–0 lead in the third inning over the Blue Jays in Toronto. The Os hung on to win, 5–4, thanks to their defense. Baltimore turned in three double plays in the game—none more spectacular than in the sixth inning.

With Toronto trailing, 5–3, Kelly Gruber and George Bell opened the sixth with singles off Orioles' starter Bob Milacki. Reliever Mark Thurmond replaced Milacki. The first batter Thurmond faced was slugger Fred McGriff, who drilled his nineteenth homer earlier in the game. This time McGriff hit a sharp grounder that was headed for right field.

Billy sprinted from his second-base position, gloved the ball, spun, and fired to Cal—who arrived at second base just before Bell. Cal hung in against Bell's hard slide, and fired to first in time to double-up McGriff. The double play was a great one, and the win was great for the Orioles. This victory gave the team a 47–34 record at the midway point of the season, and a 6 1/2-game lead in the division.

Pat Gillick, general manager of the Blue Jays, said, "Watching the Orioles is like watching a basketball team that's playing well together. Defense is a rhythm, team thing, and everyone's hustling and trying to outdo one another. It's great to watch."[5]

The Orioles lost eight straight games immediately after the All-Star break, and eventually missed the division title by two games. But the team was in first place for 116 days—a far better effort than anyone had expected. This effort was largely due to Cal Ripken. Cal never gave up in a game, and it made an impression on the new young Orioles, who began hustling on every play.

In a game against Cleveland in early September, Ripken showed his worth. The Indians were in the process of routing the Orioles, 9–0. The blowout gave manager Frank Robinson a chance to see

Ripken has become an inspiration to younger players, hustling on every play.

what his rookie pitcher, Ben McDonald, could do. With the Indians ahead, 4–0, in the top of the third, McDonald made his major league debut. With runners at first and third, one out, and Cory Snyder at the plate, Ripken hustled in from shortstop to talk to McDonald. "Make sure you come to a stop, Ben," Cal told the rookie. "Let us get the outs for you. That's what we're here for."

McDonald's first pitch was just outside to Snyder, who hit a slow bouncer up the middle. Ripken had positioned himself perfectly. He gloved the ball, and flipped to his brother to start a 6-4-3 (shortstop to second to first) double play. McDonald had recorded two outs on his first major league pitch. "I had a couple of balks in the minors, and Cal knew that," McDonald said. "I'd heard he knows the game."[6]

Cal committed just eight errors all season, and finished with the best fielding percentage of all major league shortstops. His batting was another story, however. He slugged 21 homers and drove in 93—as usual—but his average was just .257. He hit a home run April 10 off Frank Viola, but didn't hit another until April 29 against Nolan Ryan. This homerless streak, the longest of his career thus far, had lasted forty games.

Cal was so frustrated at one point in the season

that he got thrown out of a game by home plate umpire Drew Coble. In the first inning of a game against the Minnesota Twins at Memorial Stadium, Ripken complained so angrily about a strike call that Coble had to eject him. Coble said afterward, "It was like throwing God out of Sunday school."

Cal wouldn't discuss what happened at the time. Several months later, he said he felt horrible about the incident. "I didn't feel I handled it right," Cal admitted. "I was ranting and raving. It was all temper." Cal felt even worse when he learned that a boy had come up from the state of Virginia for the day, just to watch Cal play. "I got thrown out in the first inning, and the kid cried the whole game," Cal said.

On the last weekend of the season, former Orioles Brooks Robinson and Jim Palmer, two players Cal knew well, criticized his hitting on TV. "The problem I have with Cal is that he changes his stance so much," Robinson said. "He's trying to pull everything." Palmer agreed. "The man of many stances," Palmer said. "The question about Cal is, after playing all those games, is he getting tired?"[7]

Chapter 7

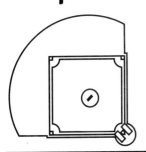

On the Upswing Again

The critics were now howling. Cal was off to a sluggish start at the plate in 1990, and fans were dialing radio call-in talk shows in the Baltimore area to criticize the veteran shortstop. They said: "He doesn't get enough RBIs." "He's not a team leader." "He needs a rest." Ripken heard the criticisms, but he chose not to argue with the fans. When former Orioles catcher Rick Dempsey suggested that Cal might benefit from an occasional day off, Ripken finally responded. "Well, I'll never know," Cal said with a serious face. "It'll never happen."[1]

When Ripken still was batting .209 in early June, the grumblings were louder than ever. Then hitting coach Tom McCraw came to Cal's aid. "I'm the batting instructor and I'm not complaining," McCraw said. "Cal is a superb athlete and a great

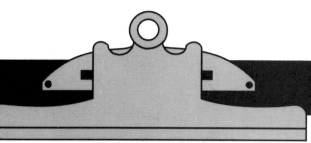

STATS

Cal proved his greatness with a baseball glove in 1990. He established the best fielding percentage in a season by a shortstop in baseball history. Even more amazing is that Cal was overlooked for the Gold Glove award that year. Here are the five best fielding years ever by a shortstop.

NAME	TEAM	YEAR	PCT	ERRORS
Cal Ripken	Orioles	1990	.996	3
Tony Fernandez	Blue Jays	1989	.992	6
Larry Bowa	Phillies	1979	.991	6
Ed Brinkman	Tigers	1972	.990	7
Cal Ripken	Orioles	1989	.990	8

pro. He'll hit. What you can't see is how Cal dominates the mental side of the game. You'd have to watch him every day, and watch him close."[2] McCraw's words made sense. After all, Cal didn't have a spectacular year at the plate in 1989 either. Yet he finished third in the voting for the American League MVP. This was because the voters understood that Cal contributes in so many ways other than just hitting.

Manager Frank Robinson dropped Ripken from third to sixth in the order, but the move didn't make much sense. None of the Orioles players were hitting well. Cal was surrounded by an inexperienced lineup. Catcher Mickey Tettleton and third baseman Craig Worthington were in deep slumps. Randy Milligan was the only other player showing any power. Ripken wasn't sure when he would start hitting again, but he was sure of this: baseball wasn't much fun in 1990. "There were times when I felt like I had to do everything myself, and that created a lot of pressure," Cal said. "It was hard to come to the park at times."[3]

With the season not going so well, Cal took the time to reflect on the game. "I feel fortunate to know the losing side," he said. "Maybe you appreciate winning more. Maybe otherwise you'd take winning for granted. Maybe you're a better person for

Ripken throws the runner out at first. He holds the record for the fewest errors by a shortstop in a season.

experiencing defeat as well as success. If you only see one side of it, you don't have the full picture."[4]

Cal began hitting again in July. But when Milligan suffered a year-ending injury in early August, Cal was unprotected in the lineup, and his batting tailed off again. He socked 21 homers and had 84 RBIs—numbers that had become automatic by now. But his batting average dipped to a career-low .250. He hit only .204 with runners in scoring position. Ripken said he was trying to do too much because the rest of the team wasn't hitting.

Almost lost in the difficult batting year was Cal's brilliant season in the field. In 161 games he made just three errors. That broke the old record for fewest errors in a full season by a shortstop, which was six. Cal handled 680 chances and misplayed just three. Brother Billy made just eight errors all season at second base. The brothers set a major league record for fewest errors—11—by a short-stop-second baseman combination.

More amazing than Cal's superb fielding season was that he didn't win the American League Gold Glove for his efforts. The Gold Glove is awarded to a player at each position by a vote of coaches. Instead of Ripken winning the award for committing just three errors, Chicago White Sox shortstop Ozzie Guillen won it, despite committing 17 errors.

"I'm embarrassed by my peers,"[5] said Texas Rangers coach Bobby Valentine, who voted for Ripken. Cal would've liked to have won a Gold Glove, but he had something more important on his mind as soon as the season ended—how to get his hitting stroke back.

During the off-season Cal worked harder than ever before. He broke down the mechanics of his swing, and with the help of manager Frank Robinson, he learned a new one. "He was on a mission," Orioles pitcher Mike Flanagan said.[6] Ripken agreed and explained his motivation. "I got away last year from what made me successful. I looked in the mirror and asked, 'Is my talent dwindling?'" That question was answered soon enough. Cal changed his stance by spreading his feet wider, resting the bat on his shoulder, and crouching down a little. "I decided to wait for the ball instead of trying to hit it before it got to me," Ripken explained. "The key to hitting is waiting as long as you can. I'm strong enough to hit the ball out. I don't need to gather all kinds of momentum."[7]

The Orioles suffered a blow early in the year when first baseman Glenn Davis got hurt. Davis was supposed to hit behind Ripken, giving Cal better pitches at which to swing. The injury didn't faze Cal. His new stance and swing worked from the start. By the All-Star Game, Cal was near the lead in the American League in almost every offensive category. The critics were silent; some even were enjoying Cal's terrific year.

The annual All-Star Game was being held in Toronto in 1991. Cal had been voted by the fans as the American League's starting shortstop for the eighth straight year. He showed up at SkyDome the day before the game for a homer-hitting contest. Barry Bonds was there, as were Darryl Strawberry, Will Clark, and Howard Johnson. Most people thought gigantic slugger Cecil Fielder of Detroit would win the contest. No one gave much thought to Ripken.

There were eight players in the contest. The other seven batters combined for 15 home runs. Ripken took 22 swings. He hit an amazing 12 homers—nearly as many as the other seven sluggers combined! He hit several balls more than 400 feet, then saved the best for last. On his last swing, he drove the ball so high and far that it landed in the fifth deck. Only mighty José Canseco had reached that deck before.

Cal continued his powerful hitting in the All-Star game the following night. With millions of viewers tuned in on TV, Cal almost single-handedly beat the National League. In the first inning he drilled a single to left field off Atlanta Braves pitcher Tom Glavine, the starter for the National League. Then in the third, with American League stars Rickey Henderson and Wade Boggs on base, Ripken came up to bat again. Cal worked Montreal Expos starter Dennis Martinez to a 2-and-1 count, and then looked for a breaking ball. Martinez came in with a slider, and Cal turned on it. He drove the ball high over the wall in left center field for a home run, giving his side a 3–1 lead. The American League went on to win the game, 4–2. Cal easily won the game's Most Valuable Player award.

Once the season resumed Ripken continued to tear into the ball. His most emotional night came late in July at Memorial Stadium. Before the game against the Seattle Mariners, Cal was presented with the van he won for being the All-Star Game MVP. Immediately he donated it to a local reading program that he had established two years earlier. He received thunderous applause both for winning the MVP and for giving away the van. Then the public address announcer informed the crowd this was Cal's 1,500th consecutive game played. This announcement triggered another roar from the crowd. In the seventh inning the Orioles trailed 1–0 when Cal came up with a runner on base. He promptly hammered Rich DeLucia's first pitch out

FACT

The Orioles finished in sixth place in 1991. But Cal had such a great season that he won the league's Most Valuable Player award. Cal became the first player in baseball history to receive this honor while playing on a losing team. Cal also won the MVP in 1983. He is just the twentieth player ever to be league MVP more than once.

When Ripken won the All-Star MVP in 1991, he donated his prize to charity.

of the park for a two-run homer to win the game, 2–1. It was Ripken's twentieth home run of the season. After the game Ripken said, "Without a doubt, this was a special night. I hold this night deep."[8]

The Orioles were never in the chase for the division title, but Cal finished with his best individual season ever. He had career highs in batting average, with .323; home runs, with 34; and RBIs, with 114. He became the eighth player to slug 20 or more home runs in each of his first 10 full seasons. He led the majors in multi-hit games, extra-base hits, and total bases. He was the only American Leaguer to rank in the top 10 in hits, average, doubles, homers, RBIs, and slugging percentage. In the field Cal led the league in fielding percentage for the second straight year, led chances and putouts for the fourth time, double plays for the fifth time, and assists for the sixth. He was also finally awarded the Gold Glove—an honor he deserved in previous seasons.

Despite all that Ripken didn't believe he had a chance at his second league MVP award. "The MVP is for someone who has helped his team win," he said. "There can't be a real big case for me because we didn't have a good year."[9] A few days later, it was announced that Ripken had won the award. He was thrilled. Considering how he struggled the previous year, he deserved to be proud. "To rebound and have a really good year makes this very special to me," he said. "I appreciate it very much. I tried to downplay it, but I'm very excited."[10]

The end of Cal's amazing 1991 season also marked the end of an era for Orioles fans. Memorial Stadium in Baltimore would no longer be used by the team for baseball. A new park would be the Orioles home beginning in 1992. The club couldn't decide whether to name it Oriole Park or Camden

In 1991 Ripken won the Gold Glove, an award given to the best player at each position.

FACT

On October 6, 1991, at 5:07 P.M., Cal made history in an unfortunate way. He had the dubious honor of being the last player ever to bat in Memorial Stadium history when he bounced into a 6–4–3 (shortstop to second to first) double play off Frank Tanana of the Tigers. The following year Baltimore began playing home games in Oriole Park at Camden Yards.

Yards. So it was officially named Oriole Park at Camden Yards.

During spring training, prior to the 1992 season, Cal and the Orioles often talked about the new facility. "Before, we were always going back to Memorial Stadium, so you didn't really think that much about Opening Day," Cal explained. "I'm kind of excited about seeing the new park."[11]

One week into the 1992 season Cal was struck in the left elbow by a pitch thrown by Toronto's Jack Morris. Then, right before the All-Star Game, he was drilled in the back with a pitch from Minnesota's John Smiley. Cal, at 32, noticed something about his body. The pain in his body lingered for weeks instead of disappearing within a matter of hours—or a couple of days—as it did ten years earlier. Cal had a tough time in 1992 for another reason—contract problems. Cal finally signed a lucrative five-year $30.5 million deal on August 24, but the five months of haggling affected his focus.

Whatever the reason, Ripken was having a tough year at the plate. The problem was enough to encourage new manager Johnny Oates to consider different ways he could rest Cal without disrupting his streak of consecutive games played. "I'm not big enough to end something he's worked

11 years for," Oates admitted, "but it's not so important that I can put it ahead of the team."[12] Oates talked of letting Cal bat in the first inning and then giving him the rest of the day off, or maybe using him as a designated hitter. Cal struggled through the rest of the season, finishing with a career-low in homers, with 14; and RBIs, with 72. Oates never did monkey with his veteran shortstop's duties, however.

The Orioles were in the division title chase with the Blue Jays. But down the stretch the Os lost six of seven games at home to fall five games behind the Jays in the standings. In the last of those contests, Milwaukee pitcher Cal Eldred out-dueled Orioles ace Ben McDonald. Eldred pitched a four-hit shutout as the Brewers won, 2–0. When Eldred struck out Ripken in the seventh inning, the Baltimore crowd of 44,242 booed the shortstop.

Just two days earlier the crowd had reacted differently. Cal had suffered a twisted right ankle running out a double play against the Brewers. At that time the fans had sat hushed and very concerned as Ripken limped back to the dugout. The injury was serious enough that the Orioles called up a shortstop from their Triple-A roster—just in case. Now, two days later, the crowd was booing its hero. The crowd reaction showed how easily the

FACT

In 1992 Ripken had a candy bar named after him. The "Cal Bar" was introduced by a company in Maryland. The candy is advertised as a "double play of peanuts and caramel in milk chocolate." All profits for Ripken's "Cal Bar" are donated to charity.

In 1993 Cal was selected by the fans to start at shortstop in his ninth consecutive All-Star Game. This game was more special than any other because it was played in Cal's home stadium— Oriole Park at Camden Yards. When Cal was introduced, he received a thunderous ovation from the fans that lasted several minutes. Afterward he said, "I've had a lot of great moments in my short career. This has to be number one. I can't even describe it."

mood of fans can change. A team-record 3.56 million people turned out to see the Orioles play their inaugural season in Oriole Park at Camden Yards. So most of the time, fortunately, the support was there.

Cal showed up for spring training in 1993 in a much different frame of mind than his previous dozen camps. For the first time in his career he felt lonely. "I don't know how to put my feelings into words," he said. "There's some hurt I'm having to deal with."[13] During the off-season, the Orioles had released Cal Ripken senior and Billy Ripken. Mr. Ripken had been a coach with the Orioles for 32 years. Billy hit just .230 in 1992, and the organization wanted to try someone new at second base. "I'm used to having my dad here, so that hurts," Cal said. "And I got used to having my younger brother here taking ground balls next to me. It's strange that they aren't here. I felt like I was lost when I got here."[14]

Although the Orioles were a strong team, they weren't expected to win the division in 1993. Toronto had won the World Series in 1992, and the Blue Jays just appeared to be too powerful offensively for the rest of the division. Instead the run for the title turned out to be quite a race. Toronto led most of the way, but the Orioles and the New

After more than a decade with the Orioles, Ripken is always trying to improve his batting style.

York Yankees kept pace until the very end. The Yankees and Blue Jays were tied as late as September 9. And the Orioles, who had won 10 of 11, were just 1/2 game behind. Toronto then went on a five-game winning streak to take the lead for good.

Chapter 8

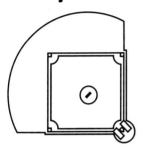

"The Perfect Story"

The tunnel at the Metrodome in Minneapolis that leads from the visitors' dugout to the club-house is long and steep—thirty-three steps separated by two landings. Every time Cal plays in Minnesota, he does the same routine. After he finishes his pre-game warm-ups he sprints off the field and runs up the stairs. The game Cal invented is to take as few steps as possible to get to the top step. "He can do it in six," Orioles manager Johnny Oates said. "It's ridiculous. It's amazing."[1] That's what Cal Ripken is all about—games, competition, doing amazing things.

"He doesn't ever want to lose, even in these tiny games," Orioles outfielder Brady Anderson said. Cal plays a game called sockball in the hallway during rain delays. It's a form of baseball with a taped-up sock. "He's sweating his butt off, trying

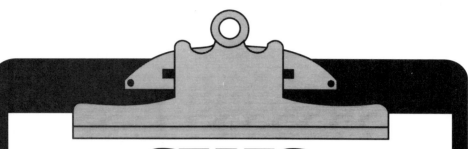

STATS

Big sluggers often come and go. But Cal has been a consistent slugger for many years. He is one of only eight players to hit twenty or more home runs in his first ten full seasons in the majors. Of the other seven sluggers, six are in the Hall of Fame. Below is a list of the players and the number of years they belted twenty or more homers.

PLAYER	YRS	PLAYER	YRS
Eddie Matthews	14	Cal Ripken	10
Billy Williams	13	Joe DiMaggio	10
Reggie Jackson	13	Ted Williams	10
Frank Robinson	12	Rocky Colavito	10

to win this tiny game," Brady explained, "then he goes out and gets two hits." At Anaheim Stadium where the Angels play, there's a stretch of dirt between the grass. After the Orioles are through with their pre-game stretches, Cal pulls Brady over to the dirt. "He and I *always* have to long-jump over the dirt," Anderson said. "He makes it, of course."[2]

The Orioles in 1993 began having autograph contests in the dugout. The way the contest works is that two players go head-to-head writing their names, to see who has the coolest handwriting. Then they bring their autographs to Cal, who

Ripken is a hero to Baltimore fans, both on and off the field.

FACT

Cal is nicknamed the "Iron Man" because he has played for so many years without missing a single game. He broke the record of Lou "The Iron Horse" Gehrig for most consecutive games played. Here is a list of the all-time greats, and their streak of games played.

1. Cal Ripken	2,478
2. Lou Gehrig	2,130
3. Everett Scott	1,307
4. Steve Garvey	1,207
5. Billy Williams	1,117
6. Joe Sewell	1,103
7. Stan Musial	895
8. Eddie Yost	829
9. Gus Suhr	822
10. Nellie Fox	796

declares the winner. The winner then advances to the next round. Cal serves as the judge every time.

Baltimore manager Johnny Oates understands the value of Ripken to the Orioles. "I dare say," the manager has often said, "that if you had 25 Cal Ripkens on your roster—and I'm not talking about ability, but attitude and approach—you'd win about 120 games a year."

Cal cares about his teammates. Sometimes before road trips to the West Coast, Cal will buy a huge batch of crabs. Then he'll have them loaded onto the plane for all the players and coaches to eat—just to be nice.

Cal cares about his health. "I'm not a junk-food addict, but I'm not a health-food nut either. I strive for a balanced diet. I include vegetables to get all the nutrients my body needs."[3]

Cal cares about the community. In 1988 he donated $250,000 to build the Ripken Learning Center, which helps adults learn to read and do math. He also contributes money to other literacy programs as well.

Most of all, Cal cares about the game of baseball. And he's honest about what he can contribute. "The hard-core reality is I'm not the type of person who can carry the team," he has said. "No one player makes a difference in baseball. In football, yes. And in basketball. In baseball you only go to bat four times a game. It's a group of individuals playing collectively as a team."[4]

Cal's biggest contribution to the game is "The Streak." In an era long ago, Lou Gehrig played in 2,130 consecutive games. Cal closed in on and surpassed the record that most thought would never be touched. "The streak symbolizes dependability," Ripken said. "I want to be in the lineup for the team. I was raised to be a team player, and I am proud of the streak. I want to be remembered for always being in the lineup, that my teammates could expect me to be there. That they could depend on me through the good times and the bad."[5]

Ripken wants to be remembered most for never letting his teammates down.

To break Gehrig's legendary record Cal needed to stay injury-free and play every day. With the world watching during the summer of 1995, Cal played through what must have seemed the longest season of his life. Finally, on September 6, 1995, Cal walked out onto the Orioles home field and started his 2,131st consecutive game before a crowd of 46,000 that included President Clinton. Gehrig's record was broken!

Despite Ripken's heroic efforts the Orioles finished the 1995 season in third place, 71–73. The Orioles rebounded in 1996. Baltimore finished second in the AL East, 88–74, good enough for a wild card berth. Ripken played a large part, finishing with 26 home runs and 102 runs batted in and continuing to play every game in the field. The Orioles defeated the Cleveland Indians, 3–1 in the Divisional Series, but lost to the Yankees 4–1 in the AL Championship Series.

The Orioles decided to make some changes in 1997. Manager Davey Johnson felt the team would

Ripken's love and enthusiasm for the game has made him one of the greatest players in the history of baseball.

be more competitive with Ripken moving to third base. Ripken is a team player and went along with the move. The Orioles benefitted from the change and finished in first place in the AL East, 98–64. This time Cleveland beat the Orioles four games to one to win the AL title. Ripken hopes to lead the Orioles back to the playoffs in 1998.

How is it that Cal Ripken came to be the way he is? Why is he so generous? Why does he never get hurt? Oates thinks he knows. "He's like a twelve-year-old kid who happens to be very good," Oates said. He continued:

> When I was 12 years old and playing Little League, I couldn't wait to put on my uniform. When we had a game, I'd wear my uniform to school. By the time I got to the field, I had mustard on my shirt and ketchup on my pants. I couldn't wait to play. And that's the way Cal comes to the park every day. He knows how to have fun, and he takes that enthusiasm on the field with him every game. He doesn't do it with a lot of flash. He doesn't run around high-fiving everybody. If he hits a home run, he goes around the bases like he doesn't want anybody to notice. He doesn't worry about contracts. He just plays the game.[6]

Orioles' public relations director Bob Miller said of Cal: "He's a good husband, a good father, and his teammates like him. He's the American boyhood dream—the star player in his hometown. He's just the perfect story."[7]

Notes
by Chapter

Chapter 1

1. Mark Maske, "Steady Cal Ripken Swings into High Gear," *Washington Post* (June 25, 1991), pp. 1–3.

2. John Delcos, "The Ripkens: Cal Sr. & Jr. & Billy," *Diamond* (May/June 1992), pp. 11–15.

3. Tim Kurkjian, "Rip on a Tear," *Sports Illustrated* (August 1991), pp. 24–29.

4. Ross Newhan, "No Surprises—Orioles' Ripken Has Become Baseball's Most Enduring Star by Staying Prepared," *Los Angeles Times* (March 29, 1992), p. 1.

5. Telephone interview with Cal Ripken, Jr.

6. Telephone interview with Cal Ripken, Jr.

Chapter 2

1. Tim Kurkjian, "Rip on a Tear,"*Sports Illustrated* (August 1991), pp. 24–29.

2. Patrick A. McGuire, "The Man Behind the Iron Man Image," *Orioles Magazine* (March 25, 1990), pp. 9–13.

3. Tim Kurkjian, "Baseball's First Family," *Baltimore Sun* (March 1, 1987), pp. 19–22.

4. Ibid.

5. Kurkjian, "Rip on a Tear," pp. 24–29.

6. Kurkjian, "Cal and the Streak," *Sports Illustrated* (June 1990), pp. 72–80.

7. Newhan, p. 1.

8. Kurkjian, "Baseball's First Family," pp. 19–22.

9. Jan Schleifer, "Cal Ripken—One of the Good Guys," *Listen* (May 1986), pp. 16–19.

10. Ibid.

11. Kurkjian, "Cal and the Streak," pp. 72–80.

12. Schleifer, pp. 16–19.

13. Kurkjian, "Baseball's First Family," pp. 19–22.

14. Thomas Boswell, "Cal Ripken Jr. Is the Best Baseball Player Alive. Period," *Gentleman's Quarterly* (April 1985), pp. 208–211, 284.

15. Mark Maske, "Steady Cal Ripken Swings into High Gear," *Washington Post* (June 25, 1991), pp. 1–3.

Chapter 3

1. Telephone interview with Cal Ripken, Jr.

2. Patrick A. McGuire, "The Man Behind the Iron Man Image," *Orioles Magazine* (March 25, 1990), pp. 9–13.

3. Telephone interview with Cal Ripken, Jr.

4. Eddie Crane, "Pitcher Ripken Finishes in Style," *Washington Star* (June 8, 1978) p. 6.

5. Ibid.

6. Bryan Burwell, "Ripken, Orioles' No. 2 Draft Choice, Fans 17 as Aberdeen Wins Class A Title," *Baltimore Sun* (June 8, 1978) p. 4.

7. Crane, p. 6.

8. Ibid.

Chapter 4

1. Jim Henneman, "Let 'er Rip," *Baltimore Sun* (April 5, 1992), pp. 1–2.

2. Bryan Burwell, "Ripken, Norris Go To School in Rookie League," *Baltimore Sun* (July 31, 1978), p. 1.

3. Bob Hertzel, "Cal Ripken Redefines the Art of the Classic Shortstop," *Baseball Digest* (December 1983), p. 47.

4. Seymour S. Smith, "Ripken Is Wise to Torrid Start," *Baltimore Sun* (April 29, 1980), p. 1.

5. Bill Koenig, "Ripken's 3 Homers Tear Up Charleston," *Rochester Times-Union* (April 28, 1981), p. 1.

6. Edward Kiersh, "Baseball's New Iron Man Keeps It Simple," *VisaVis* (May 1992), pp. 57–58.

7. Glen Macnow, *Sports Great Cal Ripken, Jr.* (Hillside, N.J.: Enslow Publishers, Inc.), p. 22.

8. George F. Will, *Men At Work—The Craft of Baseball* (New York: Macmillan Publishing Company, 1990), pp. 231–291.

9. Thomas Boswell, "Cal Ripken Jr. Is the Best Baseball Player Alive. Period," *Gentleman's Quarterly* (April 1985), pp. 208–211, 284.

10. Patrick A. McGuire, "The Man Behind the Iron Man Image," *Orioles Magazine* (March 25, 1990), pp. 9–13.

11. Ibid.

12. Ibid.

13. Bob Maisel, "Success Hasn't Spoiled Young Cal the Least Bit," *Baltimore Sun* (November 25, 1982), p. 1.

14. Ibid.

Chapter 5

1. Bob Hertzel, "Cal Ripken Redefines the Art of the Classic Shortstop," *Baseball Digest* (December 1983), p. 47.

2. Thomas Boswell, "Cal Ripken Jr. Is the Best Baseball Player Alive. Period," *Gentleman's Quarterly* (April 1985), pp. 208–211, 284.

3. Patrick A. McGuire, "The Man Behind the Iron Man Image," *Orioles Magazine* (March 25, 1990), pp. 9–13.

4. Boswell, pp. 208–211, 284.

5. Tim Kurkjian, "Cal and the Streak," *Sports Illustrated* (June 1990), pp. 72–80.

6. Boswell, pp. 208–211, 284.

7. Jan Schleifer, "Cal Ripken—One of the Good Guys," *Listen* (May 1986), pp. 16–19.

8. Ibid.

9. Hank Herman, "Count on Cal," *Men's Health* (June 1992), pp. 54–57.

10. Ibid.

11. Schleifer, pp. 16–19.

12. Tim Kurkjian, "Baseball's First Family," *Baltimore Sun* (March 1, 1987), pp. 19–22.

13. Ibid.

14. Ibid.

Chapter 6

1. George F. Will, *Men At Work—The Craft of Baseball*

(New York: Macmillan Publishing Company, 1990), pp. 231–291.

2. Jan Schleifer, "Cal Ripken—One of the Good Guys," *Listen* (May 1986), pp. 16–19.

3. Tim Kurkjian, "Cal and the Streak," *Sports Illustrated* (June 1990), pp. 72–80.

4. Ibid.

5. Will, pp. 231–291.

6. Kurkjian, pp. 72–80.

7. Ibid.

Chapter 7

1. Tim Kurkjian, "Cal and the Streak," *Sports Illustrated* (June 1990), pp. 72–80.

2. Ibid.

3. John Delcos, "The Ripkens: Cal Sr. & Jr. & Billy," *Diamond* (May/June 1992), pp. 11–15.

4. Patrick A. McGuire, "The Man Behind the Iron Man Image," *Orioles Magazine* (March 25, 1990), pp. 9–13.

5. Tim Kurkjian, "Rip on a Tear," *Sports Illustrated* (August 1991), pp. 24–29.

6. Ibid.

7. Tim Kurkjian, "Inside Baseball," *Sports Illustrated* (May 1991), p. 62.

8. Kurkjian, "Rip on a Tear," pp. 24–29.

9. Delcos, pp. 11–15.

10. Ibid.

11. Jim Henneman, "Let 'er Rip," *Baltimore Sun* (April 5, 1992), pp. 1–2.

12. Tim Kurkjian, "Slip Slidin' Away," *Sports Illustrated* (September 1992), pp. 30–32.

13. Bill Center, "Cal Feels Odd as Only Ripken," *San Diego Union-Tribune* (March 20, 1993), p. 1.

14. Ibid.

Chapter 8

1. Tim Kurkjian, "Rip on a Tear," *Sports Illustrated* (August 1991), pp. 24–29.

2. Ibid.

3. Jan Schleifer, "Cal Ripken—One of the Good Guys," *Listen* (May 1986), pp. 16–19.

4. Patrick A. McGuire, "The Man Behind the Iron Man Image," *Orioles Magazine* (March 25, 1990), pp. 9–13.

5. Edward Kiersh, "Baseball's New Iron Man Keeps It Simple," *VisaVis* (May 1992), pp. 57–58.

6. Jim Henneman, "Let 'er Rip," *Baltimore Sun* (April 5, 1992), pp. 1–2.

7. Telephone interview with Cal Ripken, Jr.

Career Statistics

Year	Team	G	AB	R	H	2b	3b	HR	RBI	SB	Avg
1981	Orioles	23	39	1	5	0	0	0	0	0	.128
1982	Orioles	160	598	90	158	32	5	28	93	3	.264
1983	Orioles	162	663	121	211	47	2	27	102	0	.318
1984	Orioles	162	641	103	195	37	7	27	86	2	.304
1985	Orioles	161	642	116	181	32	5	26	110	2	.282
1986	Orioles	162	627	98	177	35	1	25	81	4	.282
1987	Orioles	162	624	97	157	28	3	27	98	3	.252
1988	Orioles	161	575	87	152	25	1	23	81	2	.264
1989	Orioles	162	646	80	166	30	0	21	93	3	.257
1990	Orioles	161	600	78	150	28	4	21	84	3	.250
1991	Orioles	162	650	99	210	46	5	34	114	6	.323
1992	Orioles	162	637	73	160	29	1	14	72	4	.251
1993	Orioles	162	641	87	165	26	3	24	90	1	.257
1994	Orioles	112	444	71	140	19	3	13	75	1	.315
1995	Orioles	144	550	71	144	33	2	17	88	0	.262
1996	Orioles	163	640	94	178	40	1	26	102	1	.278
1997	Orioles	162	615	79	166	30	0	17	84	1	.270
TOTALS		2,543	9,832	1,445	2,715	517	43	370	1,453	36	.276

Where to Write
Cal Ripken, Jr.:

Mr. Cal Ripken, Jr.
c/o Baltimore Orioles
Oriole Park at Camden Yards
333 West Camden Street
Baltimore, MD 21201

Website:

http://www.totalbaseball.com/story/person/player/r/ripkc001/ripkc001.htm

Index